28 Day *Story Structure* Challenge

M.H. Salter

Daytime Moon Publishing

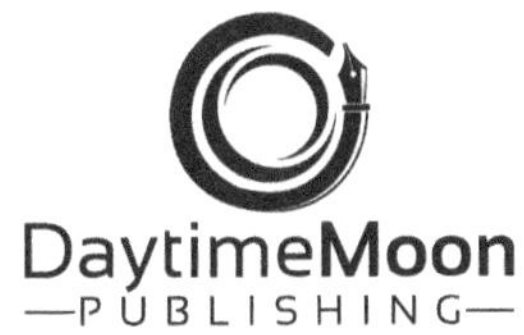

Published by Daytime Moon Publishing, South Australia

Excerpts from *Dove* by M.H. Salter 2016

ISBN: 978-1-7644438-6-9

Contact the author at <u>the.excited.writer.is@gmail.com</u>

Introduction

Hello, Writer!

Welcome to this 28 Day Challenge for writers struggling with character development.

By working through the daily lessons and writing exercises around story structure, you can bring your plot ideas onto the page as bright and shiny as you always imagined it to be.

Aside from the physical act of writing, this challenge has a second purpose. One that is even more important. It is designed to inspire and motivate you and, most importantly, increase your belief in yourself as an artist. If you don't already consider yourself a "writer" or an "artist", then I have news for you: the fact that you are either considering this challenge — or have already signed up for it — proves that you *are* a writer because you are aiming to improve on your craft. That in itself shows that you consider yourself, and your artistic merits to be worthy.

According to science, it takes an average of 21 days to form a new habit by implementing a daily practice. It takes a following 90 days to make it into a permanent lifestyle change. This 28 Day Challenge is designed to help you incorporate writing time into your life in order for it to become routine. Over these 28 days you will learn to make yourself and your writing a priority, carve out a daily routine that can become a habit, and lead you toward a MS of which you will be proud and excited to put out into the waiting world.

In the *Story Structure* Challenge, you will receive a daily lesson focusing on a different aspect of structuring your novel's storyline:

- The Beginning, The Middle, and The End and the 15 Beats within them
- Creating conflict to prevent a "saggy middle"
- Making sure every chapter is necessary
- Making sure every chapter has a strong beginning and ending
- World building tips and techniques
- Looking at what makes a great synopsis
- and getting excited, and staying excited, about your work-in-progress

So many of us will start a project, get about a third of the way through, and stop. I believe writing a novel is a cumulative process. You need to gather enough momentum (ie. excitement) at the beginning, so that when you hit those downhill slumps of self-doubt and writer's block, you will have enough inertia to get you through to actually completing your first draft. Each of these 28 day writing challenges will help you to get — and *stay* — excited about your work-in-progress.

Each daily practice contains simple, bite-sized snippets and exercises that you can either ponder on for the day and make some notes before bed, or just do in a few minutes over your morning coffee, so that even those of us who *can't* find time to write can still get something out of it. At the end of the 28 days, even if you only spent ten minutes per day on a challenge, you will end up with *four and a half hours* of writing time that you wouldn't have completed ordinarily. If you only manage a hundred words a day, by the end of the challenge you'll be *2,800 words down*! That's basically a chapter a month if you keep it up.

Remember, with this challenge, you will only get out what you put in. Allow yourself just ten minutes a day. Invest in yourself.

These daily lessons and exercises are taken from my book: *The Excited Writer*. Once this challenge is complete, you are invited to purchase the full book for even more lessons and exercises, take up another 28 Day Challenge in a specific area, or even opt to work with me one-on-one via an assessment or mentorship.

Remember, a habit takes an average of 21 days to form, and a following 90 days to become a permanent lifestyle change. Whether you finish one 28 day course and start another right away, or just continue on your own, please keep up the daily routine — even just ten minutes a day — because you are worth it.

So let's give the reader a reason to care about your characters — all of them. Show us they are human. They make mistakes. They want to be better. They hope. Your job is to make the reader *care*. And then, don't relax that grip-hold on your reader's heart.

This challenge may not have you completing your novel in 28 days, that is not the point of it. The point, my friend, is to carve out for you a new daily habit. I am honoured to be a part of your personal writing journey. Thank you for including me on the ride!

Warm regards,
Melanie Hyland Salter
(M.H. Salter)

Day One: The Beginning Bit

All great stories have the same formula: Exciting beginning, rising middle, and climactic ending. Whether you plan every plot point before even writing the first chapter, or you write by the seat of your pants and let the story take you wherever it wants to go, the story needs to go through a range of tension-ascending techniques, building to a climax, followed by a satisfying resolution. Over these four weeks we will be looking at 15 beats designed to keep your reader along for the entire ride.

But before we dive into the first act, the first five beats, and ways to make your story more exciting, we are going to look at heart of the book, and what makes this book special.

Every story has a core value that runs underneath the main storyline, and this core value, or theme, is the lesson that the main characters will learn through the course of the book. It is also the lesson that the *reader* will tale away as well.

And in order for this theme, or core value to be something that resonates with a reader, it needs to first resonate with *you*. It needs to be something that excites you.

If you are excited about what you are writing about then that energy will flow out the ends of your fingers, into the manuscript, and then back up into the reader.

As creative people, we have ideas that flit through our minds every day. So what was it about this particular idea that grabbed hold of you and made you start writing. Go back in time. Remember where you were when you got the idea for this book. Remember the inspiration. Remember the feelings that built up within you as you started picturing the characters that would be involved.

Sit in that energy for a beat. And then…

<u>Exercise: 15 min</u>

1. Write a stream of consciousness paragraph for each of the following:

    The original story concept excited me because:

    ____

    ____

    ____

    ____

    ____

    What lesson is your main character (and therefore your reader) going to learn?

    ____

    ____

    ____

    ____

    Why is this lesson personal and important to you?

    ____

    ____

    ____

    ____

____

____

____

____

2. Rewrite each paragraph to fit somewhere within
    your manuscript's narrative.

Day Two: Opening Image

You know the saying: *a picture is worth a thousand words*. Well, the first beat is quick but memorable. A paragraph-length snapshot, most likely in the first page of your book, possibly using metaphor or symbolism, that gives the reader an idea of *who* the character is at the beginning.

NOTE: This image will be directly contrasted at the end of the book against a final image.

Exercise: 15 min

1. Choose a symbol or metaphor that relates to your book's theme or lesson.

    ____

    ____

2. Write a short scene incorporating this metaphor or symbol that gives the reader an idea of who the character is now, before they embark on their transformative journey. You can use this symbolic image throughout the book to highlight the character's transformation.

Day Three: Theme Stated

At some point at the beginning of your book, there will be a scene in which your main character is handed their answer on a silver platter. This can come through in any form imaginable: a direct conversation with another character, a dream, a billboard message, anything at all. The point of this scene, however, is that they are told exactly what they need to learn in order to fix all their problems, and they will blatantly disregard this knowledge. The reason being is that they need to learn this lesson on their own.

In this beat, your theme (or lesson) is literally spelled out to your character. They are told that what they actually need is this specific thing. But they disregard it completely.

Exercise: 15 min

Write a short scene in which your character is blatantly told what they *need to learn* in order to obtain happiness.

This statement is the entire point of the book, and the thing they need to learn. This could be a direct conversation with another character, or something more subtle, like a slogan on a billboard. Once the character receives this message, they disregard it completely.

Day Four: The Normal World

This is the life your characters live before the story kicks into gear and their world is turned upside-down.

This is where you briefly introduce the main characters, and hint at the problems that need to be addressed, whether the characters are aware of them or not.

Exercise: 15 min

Briefly introduce the main character's usual way of life, using this normality to hint at the problems that need to be addressed. If things don't change, then they will never transform. They will stay exactly as they are now. And that is *not* a good thing.

____

____

____

____

____

____

____

____

Day Five: The Inciting Incident

Sometimes referred to as the catalyst, this is the point where your characters' lives are interrupted by something BIG. It disrupts their normal life, and prevents the character from being able to continue living life the way they previously were.

Exercise: 15 min

What is the catalyst that interrupts your character's "normal life"? Why can they no longer continue on as they are? What will happen to them if they do not act on this?

____

____

____

____

____

____

____

____

____

____

Day Six: The Debate

Because of the inciting incident, your characters will find themselves at a fork in the road, and will be forced to make a decision. Either way, from this point, their lives will never be the same again.

Exercise: 15 min

Write a scene in which your character realises they need to make a decision. Have them weigh up the pros and cons of this decision. Have them realise that no matter which decision they make, they can never go back to their "normal life".

____

____

____

____

____

____

____

____

____

____

Day Seven: The Beginning Bit Conclusion

If you've just gone a full week of writing every day, filled out your basic plan for Act One, and taken a huge step in fleshing out your current work in progress, well friggin' done! I am *so* proud of you.

And if you maybe missed a few lessons, or not completed the exercises, that's okay too; these practices aren't going anywhere and you can go back to any one of them whenever you want. I am still so proud of you, because you are still here, and you are still showing up for yourself!

Remember, however fast or slow you go is okay. Congratulate yourself for being here in the first place.

You've now got at least a plan for the whole beginning of your book, and I wanted to take a bit of time here to talk about backstory.

Backstory is everything that has happened to your character prior to your first chapter. Backstory is the reason why your character is starting his or her story in the exact place where chapter one begins. Backstory is the reason why your character is the way they are. Backstory gives your characters depth, and it should be used in small measure to bring all of this out.

Using backstory in your beginning is a great way to give the reader a glimpse (using "show don't tell") of your character's faults or wounds, and causes them to wonder if the character will be about to complete this transformation and heal themselves by the end of the book.

However…

The full backstory should *NOT* appear anywhere in chapter one. Ever. Using a full descriptive backstory will — funnily enough — take the reader *back*. Therefore the story will no longer move *forward*, and that is something you must avoid until the inertia of your plot is well-established.

For example, in the first chapter of my book, *Dove*, Ray alludes to a piece of her backstory that the reader will not learn until Chapter 47, and in the lead up to this revelation, the story is sprinkled with crumbs of curiosity in order to draw out the tension of her deadly secret.

Of course, I'd never told [Japhy] about what I'd done. He didn't know that my soul was shredded. He didn't know that killing someone rips a hole right through you. And if I have anything to do with it, he will never know how it feels to have somebody else's death ingrained into your very being, as much a part of who you are as is your blood cells and eyelids and yesterdays. [...] They say that killing during war is heroic, but you can't mend a shredded soul with a war medal. I knew about these things. And because I knew about them, I would make sure that Japhy never had to; his soul will stay as pure and white as mine had been, once upon a time.

Use your backstory to *hint* at who your character is, what drives them, what they are capable of, what are they most afraid of, or something they plan to never reveal to anyone.

<u>**Exercise: 15 min**</u>

1. What is a significant life event took place prior to
    chapter one that still causes your character a strong
    emotion, such as regret, horror, fear, shock, etc?

____

____

____

____

____

____

____

____

____

____

____

____

____

____

2. Write a short paragraph in which your character *hints* about this event and the feelings or worries it brings up, focusing more on the emotional conflict it causes.

3. Write a "final reveal" scene to be inserted in the
manuscript in a later point.

Day Eight: The Middle Bit

You're about to start working on the middle of your book, and this where you can run into danger of the dreaded "Sagging Middle Syndrome."

So how do you make sure that you don't slow the pace and let the reader's mind wander to things like whether or not they stacked the dishwasher?

Conflict. Create conflict in every single scene.

Every.

Single.

Scene.

One surefire way to heighten the pace of the book is through the use of internal conflict. Having a character pulled in two different directions at once creates massive tension for the reader.

Every character has something they desperately want, and this is where we dive deep and use these desires to our advantage. It is now your job as the godlike-writer and omnipresent masochist that you are to analyse what this desire is. To work out what the exact *opposite* of this desire would be. And to then work out how the hell this character can also want *that* opposite desire just as badly. This is where your delicious conflict will come from.

Example: my book *Dove* opens with the female narrator, Ray, hitchhiking to Canada with her boyfriend, Japhy, to escape his draft into the army and the Vietnam War. (The arrival of his draft letter is The Inciting Incident). Ray has given up her whole world in order to go with Japhy, and obviously, the thing she wants most at this point is for him to reach the border and safely avoid the draft. Yet, she keeps catching herself guiltily wishing she could stay in the USA, and go to university, and make something of her life.

Likewise, Japhy, a pacifist, doesn't want to fight, kill, or die — hence the reason he is heading for the border. However, knowing innocent people are being injured and killed in Vietnam, and that if he joins the army perhaps he could save some of these people, makes him *want* to go and fight. He then feels guilty and cowardly for running away. These inner conflicts are the basis of every scene in the first half of my novel.

<u>Exercise: 10 min</u>

1. Write a list of your character's main five desires.

____

____

____

____

____

2. For each desire, write down its exact opposite.

____

____

____

____

____

3. Write some notes as to how this character can justify also wanting that opposite desire at the same time.

____

____

____

____

Day Nine: Act Two Begins

Because of the last beat, The Debate, your characters have now made their choice, and will have been somewhat changed as a result.

They set off on their journey toward the physical goal they *believe* will fix everything.

Exercise: 15 min

Write a scene in which your character has decided on their physical goal. What do they believe they will achieve internally once they achieve this? And how do feel about this new path?

____

____

____

____

____

____

____

____

____

Day Ten: The Upside-Down

Having started along the path toward this physical goal, and their world has been turned upside-down, the character usually meets up with a new set of characters who will help (or hinder) them on their journey.

Exercise: 15 min

Now that your character has taken the first steps on their journey, write some notes on the new set of characters they will meet, and how each one will help (or hinder) them on their journey.

____

____

____

____

____

____

____

____

____

____

____

Day Eleven: Fun and Games

This is essentially the premise of the book, and shows how your character plans to achieve their physical goal, and the steps they must take to do so. It is usually the longest part of the book.

Exercise: 15 min

1. Write down four different steps that your character will undergo on the path to achieving this physical goal leading up to the midpoint of the book.

____

____

____

____

____

____

____

____

____

____

2. Write a scene in which your character finally achieves their physical goal. How do they feel in this moment?

Day Twelve: The Midpoint (or the Second Inciting Incident)

Now that they have achieved the very thing they set out to achieve, everything should all be fine now, right? Wrong.

Plot twist. Something BIG happens to interrupt everything, and basically turns things upside-down, again. This is usually the point where the main character realises their physical goal isn't what they believed it to be.

It is a *second* inciting incident.

This should be unexpected, yet probable, and of course, completely devastating to all involved. This will force the character to question their physical goal.

<u>Exercise: 15 min</u>

Write a scene in which they realise (shock horror) that the physical goal they spent all this time seeking will *not* actually bring them the peace they thought it would.

Day Thirteen: Everything Hits the Fan

This is the downward spiral. Everything starts to go wrong. This is a mirror image of the Fun and Games Beat where everything that was built up starts to fall apart.

This can take place either in the external world, with antagonistic characters thwarting the protagonist at every turn, or in the internal world, with the protagonist self-sabotaging themself and destroying their own progress via bad choices over and over again.

Exercise: 15 min

Write some notes on the different ways that *show* how and why the physical goal will not bring happiness.

____

____

____

____

____

____

____

Day Fourteen: The Middle Bit Conclusion

You've made it to the two-week mark! Well done. How do you feel? You are now officially half way to making writing a daily practice for life.

Today is an Integration Day.

Being our last day on Act Two before we move into Act Three, I want you to integrate what you have learned and spend the time working on your work in progress to fill out your storyline by focusing on the theme and the different beats we have looked at so far.

It's all well and good to read books on structure and how to build story, but unless you actually put this into practice and integrate it into your writing, it will drop away.

So go.
Do.
Write!

<u>**Exercise: 15 min**</u>

1. Set a timer for 15 minutes and write a new scene that incorporates one of the beats covered this week.

2. Increase the pace by ending this scene with an emotional *slap!* Use this as a chapter ending.

Day Fifteen: The End Bit

Welcome to week three! Look at you go! I'm so proud of you for making time for yourself throughout this challenge. Take a moment right now to look back at the amount of work you have done on your work-in-progress throughout this challenge so far.

However much you have done, give yourself credit — it's more than you would have done otherwise, right? And that is something to be proud of.

Okay, now that we have looked at your theme and your Beginning and Middle, this week we will be looking at the End, which is where the whole thing has been leading to, the climax.

A great ending is something that a reader will not see coming, yet if they think back over the journey that they have just taken, they will notice a line of breadcrumbs leading them to this exact spot. When the ending arrives, they realise it was inevitable, no matter how unexpected it may have seemed.

<u>Exercise: 15 min</u>

1. What are *three* different outcomes for this book?

2.   Write some notes about *six* points in your manuscript where you can hint about each of these events.

Day Sixteen: Death

This is where the character experiences the death of their own flaw. They finally let it go. They overcome their false belief system. Their old, flawed self dies.

Exercise: 15 min

Write a scene in which your character reacts to a situation that *shows* their false belief has been healed. The character they were at the beginning no longer exists.

____

____

____

____

____

____

____

____

____

____

Day Seventeen: The Awakening

Because of the death, the character reflects on what they have learned, on how the life lesson or theme needs to be attained, and is now reborn into a new version of themselves, with a new determination and a new emotional goal.

NOTE: As a mirror to this scene, there will come a point near the end of your book, where your character will finally realise this lesson for themselves, realise that they had the answer all along, if they had listened at the start then they would have avoided all this drama but are grateful for what the drama has been able to teach them.

Exercise: 15 min

1. Remember Day Three: *Theme Stated — In this beat, your theme (or main character's emotional need) is literally spelled out to your character. They disregard it completely.*

   Write a scene in which the character realises the theme of the book, and reflects back on the moment where an earlier character tried to tell them what their emotional need was.

They now realise this needs to be their new goal.

Day Eighteen: The New Plan

The newly awakened character makes a plan on how to achieve this new emotional goal.

Exercise: 15 min

What is their new emotional goal? Write out a minimum of five actions they will need to do in order to achieve this new emotional goal. Which of these points are they aware of at this time in the story, and which of them will be discovered as they go along.

____

____

____

____

____

____

____

____

____

____

____

Day Nineteen: Climax

The character makes a last ditch effort to achieve their emotional goal, and they either succeed or fail (depending on your genre).

Conflict and tensions rise to this final, ultimate peak. The highest peak in the story. The climax. Everything has been leading up to this one major confrontation. Someone will win, and someone will lose.

Exercise: 15 min

1. Go through your book's outline and make a list of every subplot or loose end, and then write in the conclusion this needs.

____

____

____

____

____

____

____

____

2. How can you wrap up *all* of these subplots in one major climax. Using your list of subplots and their endings, brainstorm how these can all come together in a final explosion of wow-factor.

Day Twenty: Resolution

Your characters pick up the pieces of their lives (if they came out alive, that is). This beat contains a closing image, a new metaphorical snapshot of the book's theme that shows how the character has changed, and how life will be for them now.

NOTE: It should contrast against the Day Two: The Opening Image. This is where the loose ends are tied, and the reader says goodbye.

Exercise: 15 min

Your character has either achieved the emotional goal now, or has accepted they will never achieve this goal. Write a scene in which your character is reflecting on how their lives have changed since the start of the story. Use a closing image, a metaphorical snapshot of the book's theme that shows how the character has changed. Mirror the opening image we looked at in Day Three

____

____

____

____

Day Twenty-One: The End Conclusion

You've made it to Day 21! This is an important milestone for you. According to science, if you have implemented writing into your routine every day for 21 days, you have made it a *habit*. They say now, if you continue this for a further 90 days, it will become a permanent lifestyle change.

This week we looked at The End Bit and how your climax and ending will take place, which means you should now a completed outline of your book, as well (hopefully) as quite a lot of scenes to insert.

Today we are going to look at the narrative voice of your book and how you can make this as tight and possible.

One element that can raise your narrative voice is the use of *strong* verbs. The verb "to be" — I *am*, he *is*, they *are*, etc, — is one area that is underused in writing voice.

For example, you may have written: "he *was* walking". *Was* is the verb in that sentence. If you reduce this back to "he *walked*" it is instantly stronger.

Better still is if you can then bump this up further to use a stronger verb than "walked", something that will also show the reader the way in which the character walked.

For example: he *shuffled,* he *stomped,* etc.

<u>Exercise: 15 min</u>

1. Read through an existing scene or chapter and highlight all the "weak" verbs you can find.

2. Strengthen as many of these as you can to convey the personality or actions of your character in that scene.

3. Use this technique as you write your first draft, and as you start the editing process once your draft is completed.

Day Twenty-Two: The Adding Sparkle Bit

You've made it to our final week! I hope you have swaths of notes, scenes and chapters that you didn't have when we began this journey together. But even if you are only coming out of this challenge with a swirl of new ideas then that is great, too. I'm so proud of you for sticking it out, believing in yourself and making this a new daily habit.

Being a writer always seems exciting at the beginning, when you are first hit with that initial idea and spark and the accompanying surge of *need* to just get writing. You sit down and hammer out a few hundred words, or maybe a few thousand, but then slowly that inertia slows a little, the words stop coming, and you realise that this gig is *hard*. Crafting a piece of art that is 100,000 words long and needs to keep a reader invested for all of those 100,000 words is *hard*. Being a writer is *hard*.

But, just like childbirth, it is also worth it. Your book is worth it. Well done for believing in yourself and for sticking it out.

Today is all about believing in yourself. Today we are going to time travel. We are going into the quantum field…

<u>Exercise: 5-10 min</u>

Sit down and write a journal entry. Date it somewhere in the future, maybe in a year's time.

Write about how great you feel because that thing you were dreaming of has just happened.

Maybe you are holding your physical book in your hand, or you just signed a seven-book contract with a major publisher, or your book is being made into a movie, or you received a six-figure advance, or you finally typed those final words: *The End*.

Dream BIG, because big things *do* happen to other people, so why can't they happen to you? They *can*. Trust me.

The important thing is to put yourself in the skin of this future version of you. Feel the excitement. Don't just describe what you're doing, describe who you are *being*.

Try and continue this practice every day. Even if you don't do the journal entries, try and get into their skin once a day and live in that future version of you, feel it, be it, and believe that it is where you are heading.

Day Twenty-Three: Chapter Reasons

Over the last three weeks, you have looked at your story arc through the 15 beats and three acts. This week we will look more closely at your story arc template by creating a chapter outline.

But not just that, we will go in the *why* of each chapter. What is the <u>necessity</u> of each chapter? What are the ways in which each chapter contributes to the <u>theme</u>? What are the ways in which each chapter adds <u>conflict</u> (either external or internal)?

Go through each of your chapters, and state for each one the necessity, the theme stated, and the conflict. If you can't find a necessary reason for a particular chapter, if you can't link it to the theme, or if there is no conflict, find a way to add it in.

NOTE: If you still *can't* find a way to include necessity, theme and conflict, then maybe this chapter could be cut completely from your manuscript.

Day Twenty-Four: Chapter Bookends

You know what it's like: you're tired and you tell yourself, "I'll just finish this chapter." But the chapter ends in such a way that you simply have no choice but to go to the next chapter. So you think, "Okay, I'll read the first line just to see what is about to happen." But the first line hooks you in again. Next thing you know you're in the middle of that chapter, and you tell yourself, "I'll just finish this chapter." And once again, that chapter ends in such a way that you simply have no choice but to go to the next chapter. Next thing you know, the sun is coming up, you haven't slept a wink, and you end up finishing the entire book.

This week we will look at the ways to use conflict, cliff-hangers, and perfectly placed rising tensions, to keep up the pace of your book in relation to your chapter beginnings and endings.

Pace is all about the reader turning pages. Make sure all your chapters start and end with a *bang!*

Pace is all about creating a delicate dance — the one-two step of the first and last lines that carry the reader away — and then finding that magic balance with the crescendo and the climax and positioning your chapter break right *between* those two peaks.

<u>Exercise: 15 min</u>

Write out each chapter's first and last lines. Make sure they are each intriguing in their own right. If any seem to lack punch, rewrite them. Spend time on each one to make sure it packs a punch.

____

____

____

____

____

____

____

____

____

____

____

____

____

Day Twenty-Five: World Building

Just as characters in your book influence other characters, the setting can also influence the character. Depending on what the character can see/smell/hear/feel, the setting can bring up within them certain memories or feelings. This can then move the story forward by influencing the character in an important way.

<u>**Exercise: 15 min**</u>

1. Take an existing scene in your book in which your character needs to make a decision [*If you don't have an existing scene, write one now.*]

   Use the setting, and the ways in which the character is either *positively* or *negatively* influenced by the setting, to bring sudden clarity or resolve to a certain situation.

2. Use this at one of your major turning points.

Day Twenty-Six: Ending Types

There a few different ways you can end your novel.

These endings might be expected depending on your genre (for example, a happy ending for a romance novel) however, you have the right as the author to play with genre conventions, and use whichever ending you feel creates the best version of your book.

<u>Happy Ending</u>: Protagonist achieves their goals, antagonist is defeated, the future is clear and bright for them to have a peaceful life.

<u>Bittersweet</u>: Protagonist gets what they need at the expense of something (or someone) else, and they are now on a path of acceptance.

<u>Tragic</u>: Protagonist does not succeed in achieving their goal, and/or does not learn the moral theme and will remain just as unhealed as they were at the beginning of the book.

<u>Twist</u>: A last minute revelation turns everything the reader thought they knew upside down.

<u>Ambiguous</u>: Aspects of the story arc are left unresolved, forcing the reader to come up with their own conclusion after the book ends.

Exercise: 15 min

Even if you already have your ending planned or written, plan a different ending for each type. Do any of these resonate more than your originally planned ending?

<u>Happy Ending</u>:

____

____

____

____

____

____

<u>Bittersweet</u>:

____

____

____

____

____

____

Tragic:

____

____

____

____

____

____

Twist:

____

____

____

____

____

____

Ambiguous:

____

____

____

____

____

____

____

Day Twenty-Seven: Synopsis

The point of the synopsis is to show that you have created a well-rounded story, that moves from beginning, to middle, to end, is able to maintain conflict and pace, and tie up loose ends with a satisfying outcome.

At approximately 500 words, and using present tense and third person, the synopsis goes into detail of the story arc, the character arc, and the theme. It states the genre, the manuscript word count, and it *does* reveal the ending.

The synopsis can be broken down into four main paragraphs.

<u>Paragraph one:</u> The character, the setting, and their Normal World. The inciting Incident, or the catalyst that makes them realise that their world will never be the same again, and in order to be truly happy and to achieve the lesson of the story (theme / emotional goal) they believe they need to achieve a certain external or physical goal.

<u>Paragraph two:</u> They set out on their journey in order to reclaim what they lost or to save what was threatened. They will face a certain amount of hardships — the Fun

and Games beat — that make up a large portion of the plot until they finally reach the physical goal they set out to achieve.

Paragraph three: At the midpoint of the book, a second inciting occurs where they realise that the physical goal was not actually what they needed in order to transform and to be happy (theme/the lesson of the book). As everything starts to crumble around them, they are now faced with a final challenge in order to achieve internal happiness — the goal/theme of the book.

Paragraph four: Climax. The character either succeeds or fails. They have been changed by the journey they have taken, and the character transformation is complete.

Exercise: 15 min

Complete the Synopsis Template for your book.

(Title)____
_________________ is a (genre)
___________________________ book of _____________
words.

Paragraph one:

____

____

____

____

____

____

____

____

____

____

____

Paragraph two:

____

____

____

____

____

____

____

____

Paragraph three:

Paragraph four:

Day Twenty-Eight: What Now?

It looks like you made it to the end. Well freaking done, my friend! I am so so *so* proud of you, and so honoured to have been a part of this month. It is my sincere hope that you have come away from this challenge with a substantial amount if words under your belt, and also a good healthy dose of inspiration to keep up the good work and keep moving forward on your writing journey.

You may be wondering, "So, now what?" Well, if you enjoyed completing this challenge, then I have a few other options for you.

If you want to continue the party, you can try out my other 28 Day Challenges and focus on a specific area of your work-in-progress.

28 Day *Novel Writing* Challenge
28 Day *Creating Characters* Challenge
28 Day *First Impressions* Challenge
28 Day *Endings and What Now* Challenge

You can even choose to work with me one-on-one, either through manuscript assessments, editing, or as a book mentor.

Contact me, or view my other books, at my website <u>MHSalter.com</u> or Amazon.

Thank you so much for taking the time to go on this journey with me.

Now, let me remind you that all great writers have something in common.

Determination.

The fact that you have put time and money into this challenge, and into yourself, proves that you *do* believe in yourself and you *are* determined to be a published writer.

Exercise: 5 min

Stand in front of a mirror and look yourself in the eyes. Place your hand on your heart and…

1. Make a promise to yourself that you will complete your novel.

2. Make a promise to yourself that you will carve out time for yourself.

3. Make a promise to yourself to just *keep at it*.

4. And make a promise to yourself to *believe* that you are a great writer.

5. Repeat this exercise *every single day*.

First Chapter Assessment

Not 100% happy with your book's opening? Not sure why your first chapter isn't quite working? Get your chapter one assessment by M.H. Salter.

Receive an in-depth analysis on what is working well — and more importantly — on what is *not* working, with suggestions on how you can remedy and improve your first chapter.

- The analysis will focus on the first line and first paragraph, as well as the last line and last paragraph and how well these work together to bookend your first chapter.

- It will look at the different types of hooks you have used and how to add more, as well as the themes in your novel's beginning, and any symbols or motifs used in conjunction with this; if there don't seem to be any, you will receive some suggestions on what could work well throughout the manuscript.

- Conflict and pace will be analysed, both internal and external, and suggestions given on ways in which these can both be heightened.

- Prologues, or any use of backstory, will be highlighted to see if this could work better at a later point by enhancing tension in the lead-up to future revelations.

After receiving your assessment via email, you can dive even deeper by booking a one hour zoom call to discuss and brainstorm your novel further, or sign up to a one-on-one mentorship with M.H. Salter.

<u>What others had to say about their Chapter One Assessment:</u>

"I think it's a wonderful chance for writers to get that push in the right direction. I loved all of it."

"Melanie's assessment was warm and conveyed just how fully my first chapter had been read and understood. My novel was at a point where I knew it needed improving but I was out of ideas and inspiration about what to change. I now have, not only ideas, but concrete exercises to help me put those ideas into reality."

"I liked how the analysis was grouped beneath headings that corresponded to the [Novel Polishing] eBook. This made it much easier for me to see where the assessor was coming from, and pair it to the advice and activities in the [Novel Polishing] Book and Workbook. There was a good level of detail in the appraisal that left no question that my chapter had been thoroughly assessed. It would have been an apprehension of mine to have parted with my money and not received an appraisal that had taken the time to help me figure out exactly what my first chapter is (or should be) doing. So, thank you."

Book your Assessment with M.H. Salter now through MHSalter.com or contact Melanie at the.excited.writer.is@gmail.com

Notes